WHO BUILT THE GREAT WALL OF CHINA?

Ancient China Books for Kids
Children's Ancient History

BABY PROFESSOR
EDUCATION KIDS

Speedy Publishing LLC

40 E. Main St. #1156

Newark, DE 19711

www.speedypublishing.com

Copyright 2017

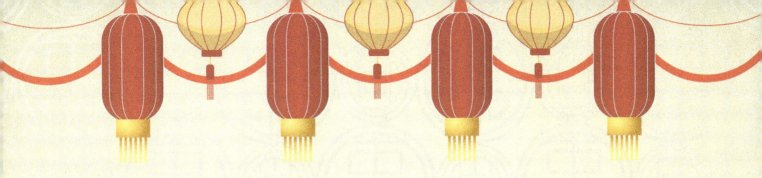

The Great Wall of China is one of the greatest engineering works in human history. Why did they build the Great Wall, and what is it like? Let's find out!

Israel–Egypt barrier

GREAT WALLS

Countries sometimes build walls to defend themselves against other countries, or to keep people from crossing into their territory. There are walls and border crossing stations between countries today, but building walls started a long time ago.

The Roman Emperor Hadrian had a wall built where England and Scotland meet, to keep the wild northern tribes out of the province of Britain. In Greece, the city of Athens built long walls to provide a safe way to travel from the city itself to its harbor at Piraeus. Denmark and Korea built similar walls for similar reasons.

The Great Wall of China is the longest, and longest-lasting, of these efforts. The wall stretches along the northern edge of China, and mainly existed to help keep China safe from attacks by armies and whole tribes from further north. The wall continued in use until one of those peoples, the Manchu, actually conquered China.

WHO BUILT THE GREAT WALL OF CHINA?

Many emperors gave orders for the wall. Many engineers designed how it should be built, and surveyors worked out exactly where it should be. But the people who actually built the wall were millions and millions of ordinary workers. They included farmers, general laborers, soldiers, slaves, criminals from prisons, and people captured from other nations during wars.

The workers had no power tools, trucks, or other aids. They had shovels, saws, buckets, and not much more. It was hard, hard work, and thousands of the laborers died before the wall was completed.

BUILDING THE WALL

In the 8th and 7th centuries BCE, there were many battles and small wars along the northern border of China. The government starting building towers, connected by short sections of wall, where the attacks were the most serious.

Eventually an emperor ordered that all the short sections of wall should be joined together into one continuous system. This was only possible because the emperor had managed to unite different parts of China into a single empire.

The Great Wall was an active part of China's defence for 2,000 years, and during most of that time it required regular labor to repair it and extend it.

LOOKING AT THE WALL

Most of the pictures we see of the Great Wall are of sections that were built or restored during the Ming Dynasty from 1368 to 1644. Other sections are much, much older and some of them are hard to find after so many years of weather and development of the country. Researchers in 2009 used range finders and GPS tools to find over 100 miles of the Great Wall that had worn down over centuries, and was concealed among hills, rivers, and more modern trenches and construction work.

The Great Wall starts at the Pacific Ocean, at Dandong and reaches all the way to Lop Lake, far to the west. Its course generally follows the southern border of Inner Mongolia. The Ming Dynasty defences are about 5,500 miles long, but the full length of all walls and defences created during all periods the Great Wall was active is more than 13,000 miles.

Some of the Great Wall is the high walls, with towers and gates, that we see in pictures. Other parts were trenches, or more simple walls. Part of the defences

made use of steep hills or rivers, where a wall was not needed to slow an attacker down.

People have said that the Great Wall is so long that you could see it if you were standing on the Moon. This is not really true, but it is a good indication of how large the Wall is in people's imaginations.

WALKING THE WALL

It is easiest to see and follow the wall going eastward from the Jiayu Pass in Gansu province. This is the west end of the Ming dynasty Great Wall. There are remains of older walls further west, but they are sometimes hard to find.

In the desert region east of the Jiayu Pass the wall splits into two sections. The Outer Great Wall is further to the north and was the main defence, while the Inner Great Wall made a second line of defence 250 miles long.

Near Beijing is the Badaling Great Wall. It was the first part of the wall to be restored and opened to the public in modern time, and is a favorite tourist destination. Since it is near Beijing, it is easier to get to than many parts of the Great Wall are. This section of the wall is over 25 feet high and 16 feet wide, and is made of stone and bricks. It was very strong to defend China's capital.

CLIMBING HILLS

Further east of Beijing, at Jinshanling, the Wall marches right up the sides of some very steep hills. This area is about seven miles long, and the wall here is between 15 and 25 feet high. To the southeast, the Mutianyu Great Wall runs between rugged mountains for almost two miles.

CROSSING WATER

At Jiumenkou is the only part of the Great Wall that was built as a bridge and crosses a river.

WHAT THE WALL IS MADE OF

The earliest parts of the Great Wall were made of piles of earth, held together with wood and some stones. The parts of the wall built during the Ming dynasty use stone, brick, tiles for roofs of structures on the top of the wall, and wood and metal for the great gates.

Stones are usually stronger than bricks, but they are also harder to work with than bricks, that come in regular shapes. So the builders used stone for the wall's foundations and the edges of the gateways, and used brick for a lot of the rest of the wall.

At the top of the wall there were battlements that defenders could fight behind, and watch towers and signal towers. These would be made of brick and wood.

On the south side of the wall there were many structures made of wood, including stables for horses, barracks for soldiers, and warehouses for supplies.

THE NAMES OF THE WALL

The first long defences north of Beijing were known as "the long walls", using the same term that we use for the walls around traditional Chinese cities. This word is actually often used to mean "city"!

In 493 CE, in The Book of Song, General Tan Daoji talks about the "long wall of 10,000 miles", and around this time the Great Wall started to be called the "Ten-Thousand-Mile Long Wall". The traditional Chinese mile was about 1,600 feet, much shorter than a mile used in Western measurement. Using "ten thousand" in the name of the Wall was like saying "the Really, Really Long Wall".

Emperors and dynasties that extended and improved the Great Wall rarely put their own names on what they had done. Instead, they used descriptions like "the frontier", "the ramparts", and "the outer fortress." Poets talked about the wall as "The Purple Frontier" and "The Dragon in the Earth."

Finally the general name "long wall" began to be used in Chinese for all the various sections of the defences. This is similar to the more common term "Great Wall" in English, French, and German. In other European languages, people talk about "the Chinese wall".

THE END OF USE OF THE GREAT WALL

The point of the Great Wall was to defend China against attacks and migrations from the north. It succeeded very well for almost two thousand years.

In the 1600s, the Ming dynasty was fighting against invasions by the Manchu from the north. The Manchus finally were able to get through the Great Wall in 1644. They had broken through the Wall several times in the past, but only to raid. This time they intended to stay.

Once the Manchus conquered China, there was no longer any point in repairing the Great Wall. The new borders of the country extended far north of the wall.

The Great Wall no longer had troops stationed along it. It fell into decline, and it was not until the middle of the 20th century that the Chinese government started to restore and preserve the Great Wall as a national treasure and a tourist attraction.

THE EFFECT OF THE GREAT WALL

The Great Wall was the greatest construction project for military defence in history, and it also helped to unite the Chinese people into one nation.

The Great Wall also controlled the flow of traffic into and out of China, and let the government tax merchants as they entered and left the country. The signal towers along the Great Wall made it much easier to send information from Beijing to parts of China thousands of miles to the west.

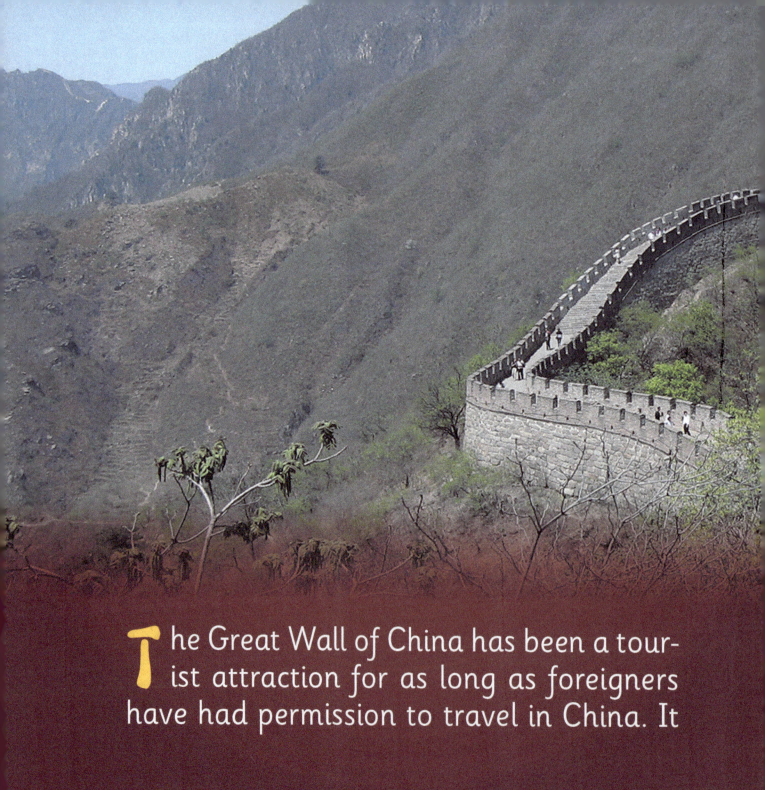

The Great Wall of China has been a tourist attraction for as long as foreigners have had permission to travel in China. It

helps people understand the great efforts China had to make in the past to become the nation it is today.

DISCOVER CHINA

China has been one of the great cultures and nations of our world. Read other Baby Professor Books, like The Chinese Festivals and Trade and Commerce in Ancient China, to learn more about this great part of the world.

Visit

BABY PROFESSOR
EDUCATION KIDS

www.BabyProfessorBooks.com

to download Free Baby Professor eBooks
and view our catalog of new and exciting
Children's Books

CPSIA information can be obtained
at www.ICGtesting.com
Printed in the USA
BVHW012255130222
628923BV00022BA/422